Speaking of the Sixties
in Verse

William X. Conlon

Speaking of the Sixties
Copyright 2021 ©
ISBN: 9798718385892
Flying Horse Press
West Haven, CT

Dedication

For Lisa, Chrissie, Marty, and Andy, children of the sixties

Take a sad song and make it better.
Paul McCartney, 1968

Table of Contents

Big Mo

Bad news reached me at work and stopped me cold.
Big Mo, close friend and cousin, now lay dead.
Freak accident resulted from some gun.
How could this be? My mind refused to deal.

At home, distraught, I could not calm myself.
I walked to homes of friends, became a pest
to everyone I saw or phoned that night.
My need to talk drove me until the dawn.

I had grand memories of all we'd done.
We fought and laughed, played ball and learned to dance.
We sneaked some smokes and drank his father's wine.
Size helped Big Mo play end on football team.

He wanted a career as a state cop
and took such pride that he made Air Police.
His roommate's gun discharged through carelessness,
Mo's life now gone before he left his teens.

Full military honors paid respect,
though tributes don't cut through such grief. I know.
We bowed our heads when soldier bugled Taps
and joined our hands to hear the rifles roar.

We watched exalted folded flag through tears,
with heartache for our airman loved as Mo.

The Playback Presents

State sent Mitchell-Ruff to Russia
with Dizzy to thaw the Cold War.
Tacked to the tree, a placard proclaimed,
"The Playback Presents Bobby Timmons."
My new love said I'd like the music of her heritage.

I took my lady to the jazz club, curious of sounds
strange for fey ears, wary of welcome
to a white youth a year shy of majority.
Not to worry, her self-assurance secured
admission. Two white couples sat in a sea
of Black at a four-top. The men wore blue
blazers and striped ties. A black tuxedoed
Black waiter walked us to our table for two.
I ordered Seven and Seven.
She sipped something sweet.

A thick man, medium height, sable skin,
purloined a nearby chair and sat with us.
Her glacial glare and steely speech preceded
her introducing her brother. He clasped
his heavy hands on the table and rumbled,
"Man, you had best be serious." I reached
my hand to him. He turned and told the waiter,
"Scotch rocks and two more for my guests."
He turned back and squeezed my hand.
I welcomed the pain.

Bobby Timmons, lately of the Jazz Messengers,
took to his "Moanin'," and the hushed room
began a subdued and rhythmic clapping,
heightened at the end of each musician's solo.
I looked at faces rapt in notes of joy.
Shared sounds of "Yeah" and "Aw'right"
told me she had told it true. I liked it.

Cuban Concern

October paints Southern Connecticut's palette
of fall foliage. Red maple leaves dance
with oaks and dogwoods in crisp breezes.
Frantic football fans sing, "Boola, boola."
College students study physics or fiction.
Our government plants bombsites in Turkey.
Russia replies with missile sites in Cuba,
sending '62 to the brink of Armageddon.

Our country readies for war when Kennedy
blockades the island. I watch and worry
for fellow students sweating ROTC status.
My student deferment diminishes my concern of conflict.
Doc Owens, physics professor, holds class at Tweed,
an airport lesson with guns to study the speed of sound.
Guns scare Doc. He shakes like an autumn
leaf in a gust. He leaves us on the tarmac.
Doc's drinking scares us. His paranoia portends
national nervousness at nuclear negation.

I glance at carefree Canada Geese lounging
by the lake and wonder if they can fly
far from the bomb. A woman walks
from Morrill Hall fingering rosary beads.
Scientists publicly pray, and I worry.

Table for Two

Our two-tone love affair fought for freedom,
a pet bird battling night's blanket,
wanting a wire to strut its stuff.
I took her to *Les Jardins,* chandeliers
and silver service, a fuck you to white
pretensions from this '60s diverse duo.

The hostess fit the format,
right out of stock-- a white woman
with white hair, wearing white clothes,
befuddled to behold my beauteous Black
angel in pearls. She marched us to a corner table
two-top in the spacious, sparsely occupied room.

My displeasure earned a larger table
near another couple at a table for four.
We shared a quiet laugh at the folly
inherent in ignorance, then ate and drank
through sharing our public show of affection.
She reveled in attention of stolen glances
from liberal New Haven's white gentry.
I shone in her ebony elegance,
magnified in the mirrored walls.

We left with my arm around her waist,
heavy with food, tipsy from drink,
giggling kids who'd filched apples from the tree,
no hiding today, our love on display.

A Dream Deferred

In sixty-three we'd dated for two years.
When seen together, we turned many heads.
At twenty-one, we had not learned to fear,
though her black skin stood out against my white.

We laughed and loved and stood against the rest.
Sometimes, we rode the train so far away.
We toured the towns and romped until the fall
when chill news told us to expect the stork.

No welcome and no joy accompanied
the news that, unwed, we should marry now.
I figured I had little left to lose
when my dad bellowed out, "No son of mine."

It did not take too long to reconcile.
How quickly parents changed and came around
to help us get our family to a start.
Let's not forget the power of a child.

Remembering now just how we set the pace,
when we risked all, that time half century past,
fills me with dread when violence borne of race
shows costly progress might not ever last.

Freedom Riders

I sit and watch the youthful crowd
chant "Black Lives Matter" to the world.
Resurgent anger, taste of bile,
recalls our righteous actions past.
We risked our lives and scorn from those
who ruled our world in ignorance.
From current news, it's obvious
the time has come to stand again.

To heed the call in '63,
we boarded buses late at night.
Well-meaning people, young and old,
not rabble rousers, Black and white,
from Dixwell Plaza, we set forth
to stand with Martin Luther King.
I chose an empty aisle seat
next to a young and pretty girl.
We sang and cheered and talked and rode
New Haven to far Washington.

Soon walking, laughing, singing song
of "We Shall Overcome Someday,"
our sore feet marched to Lincoln's shrine.
Some singers sang and preachers talked
'till Martin set us "free, at last."

Ate dinner late, caught motel sleep,
then started on our second leg.
Vowed leaving home that we would go
down South, help register to vote.
In coastal Carolina towns,
large hostile crowds surrounded us.
They yelled and cursed. They rocked our bus.
They called us commies, traitors, worse.
Stones hit some windows, shattered glass.

Blood oozing from our driver's hair
and down my seat-mate's injured cheek,
she left her seat, threw rock and shard
at hooded bigots, screaming out,
"Take that, you fools, you'll not succeed."
Our naïve plans now ripped apart,
she showed such strength instead of fear.
The driver inched through crowd until
reluctant cops came to our aid.
Against their will, they led us 'til
an opening spurred return to speed.
Police took us to highway, safe.

We headed north, and bus limped home.

November 22, 1963

To stay awake was students' main concern.
November noontime sun lulled senses with
its warmth. Professor Burns would sit and read
the text in Personality all through
the class. He droned. We dozed. Through opened door,
a runner came and walked to Doctor Burns.
She handed him a note and left the room.
He glanced at it and laid it on his desk.
I thought the note of no concern to us.
The motions toward the end of class awoke
me from my sometime sleepy fog. And then,
Professor Burns retrieved the note and read:
"A man shot JFK in Dallas, Tex."

You fool, I thought, and jumped up from my seat.
My idol bleeds while you read texts in Psych.
I ran from class out to the hall and saw
my friends and teachers hug and cry and sob.
A sprint took me outside to my wife's car.
The radio blared. She stared, then glared and dared:
"Where were you? Others have been out for long."
"Well, damn," I said, "my teacher has no heart."
She drove me home. I hung on every word
'till Cronkite said what sounded so absurd.
Saint Brendan's flamed, ablaze with votive lights.
I hoped Jack's soul had reached to greater heights.

The Hustler

Walking home, cymbal sounds of trampled
leaves of late October speak to shadows
of gibbous moon meeting neon sign announcing
Hull's beer. I glance in Yale Bowl Café,
spot the seated Mr.Tevis.

A pocket search supplies my student's need
for the fifty-cent price for two draught beers
in 1964. I hustle inside to occupy a barstool
next to the famous author. We exchange
pleasantries and converse.
He talks. I listen.

Mr. Tevis spins stories at the bar
with the same skill that marks
the street smarts of his written words.
He tells of playing pool on the road.
I see this tall buck-toothed man, an Ichabod
walk and cow-lick, shamble into local dives
to lessen the load of locals' pockets.
He talks of '51 fixes at his UK poolroom,
and I see seven-foot Spivey playing in Ansonia
before suing the NBA for a million dollars.
Moviemaking leads to tales of drinking
with Gleason at George Scott's apartment,
Liz and Richard dropping in for cocktails.

The half-dollar spent, the beer leading the way
to the john, chill air tickles my nose.
I continue home imagining myself as Fast Eddie,
imagine drinking with Liz Taylor,
imagine sitting down and writing *The Hustler*.

Five East 59th

Friend Red, his birthday near at hand,
might just book off from work that day.
"My treat, friend Red," I offered, "you
should come with me, paint New York red."

I drove my car some ninety miles,
to hit some bars and celebrate.
We took my key to Playboy Club
and settled there to hoist a few.

Red beamed and laughed and had a ball.
A few more drinks, and sure enough,
my friend let caution slip away
and tried to catch a bunny tail.

Sweet Bunny Lynn laughed not one bit.
She looked askance at Red's louche act.
Large bouncer came at her command
and gave us both the eighty-six.

We had some coffee for the drive,
which only kept this drunk awake.
Ejected from the Playboy Club,
we found our spirits somewhat low.

To vent my anger, I did drive
up Merritt Parkway carelessly.
At Housatonic Bridge, state cop
tagged me for going much too fast .

Back home, my conscience left no doubt
that we had acted like two jerks.

Innocents' Loss

Yale Divinity graduated Alan Wilson
on a bright spring Monday in '66.
Tuesday brought clouds to provide shade
for the Wilson family's packing. Their cheerful
homecoming journey to St. Louis
would commence in the afternoon.
Little Tommy wanted none of it.

Fair Tommy and our dark Lizzie sat
in the communal yard and did
whatever three year-olds do.
The inseparable tots incessantly frolicked
this past year, oblivious of their bi-racial
surroundings. Black and white and our mixed
couple comprised this planned housing co-op
in liberal New Haven's model city.

Time came for setting sail. Tommy's tears
tried to launch his parents westward without
him. He clung to Lizzie to buoy him
through his swells of sorrow. She stood
by his side, smile belying her dank eyes.
I held Lizzie's shoulders. Ann Wilson pried
her child free from his drowning embrace.

After hurried farewells, the Wilsons departed,
Tommy's tortured face flattened
against the car window. I held my stiff-spined
daughter to my leg, awed by childhood innocence.
I raked my fingers through her thick dark hair,
knowing too well that time ran short
before she learned about the spoiling construct of race.

Progress

We called ourselves Progressive Democrats,
Young Turks in the summer of '66,
set out to shake the system, grass roots
enough to give you hay fever.

Backyard barbecue fundraisers, block captains
meeting in Reverend Edmonds' church basement,
hired bus for the registration drive, no machine
would stop our push for power to the people.

Hank asked, "Why in hell is he here?"
The only white guy at Cortland's home
strategy session, I'm the one who manned
the Rolodex, made calls, counted voters.

They heaved me out of Dem HQ
when I asked for voter lists,
so the Hall of Records met my request,
and I taped the sheets to our cellar wall.

One white and nine Black men surrounded
the jug of Dewar's on primary night
and waited for wards 19 and 20 to call.
We won one, lost one, and toasted a triumph.

Against the Wall, 1967

At Carlo's, I buy smokes and turkey club.
With grinder in my hand, I cross to Moe's,
and there I buy a pint of Powers booze.
The wife and young girls left for ma's to stay
in quieter part of town. I stayed to ward
off looters at this tense and troubled time.
Black neighborhoods exploded late last night.
Brown knife, white gun brought chaos to the Hill.
For shame on Mayor Lee's prized New Haven now.
The curfew starts in minutes, and I walk.
A block from home, I'm summoned by a friend.
Old Mrs. Spencer, frail and Black, calls out.
Her worries are the August heat and more.
Race riots from last night cause her alarm.
She looks around and holds her housecoat tight.
It's after curfew when I leave her porch..

Mere yards from home, a car slams to the curb.
Four men pile out. Long guns freeze me in fear.
Cops think this white man looks for trouble here.
I raise my hands and drop the sub and freeze.
The pint's protected, in my pocket, safe.
"Don't move." "Hands up." "Turn 'round." "Against the wall."
I turn and lean against a chest-high wall.
One flashes brilliant badge. One frisks. One speaks.
The frisking makes me wish to not be seen.
"Where to? It's after curfew." "Home," I say.
"Where's that?" "Right there." I point a shaking hand.
I learn the helplessness of bullshit bust.
"Get going, fast." I leave the food and walk.
They crawl along, then speed away and leave
me at my door. The Powers stops my fright
and shakes, and it affords some peace to meet
the lonely and disturbing alien night.

Borne in the U. S. A.

April 4th, 1968, a white
man walks Henry Street, in a Black
neighborhood, to work on graveyard
shift at Winchester Repeating Arms.
Some fool killed Martin Luther King.
Silence surrounds the man's nightly
New Haven trek. No jazz seeps
from the avenue clubs. Stores cry
"soul brother" from plywood fronts, shades
of riots last summer. Dark
windows shelter neighbors from dreary
fear all share in this, Eliot's "cruelest month."
He knows his heart is heavy,
but others might only see his white
skin. Some fool did wrong.

A motorcycle breaks the hush
of his solitary shamble and focuses his dread.
A Black
man, on a black
bike, in the uniform of New Haven's finest,
comes abreast. The cop nods and drifts
ten yards back, trailing. Fear fades
with an escort and Winchester's near.
The hog turns 'round and roars down the deserted road.
The man gives a silent thanks and goes
to make munitions for the war in Asia.
Killing in the Mekong, meet killing in Memphis.

In a Righteous Place

Home from work, the day after the night
before, my thoughts centered no more.
This white man's mind reeled,
weighted with flashes of faces
processing Martin's murder in Memphis.

Some Black men stared in sullen silence.
Some snapped their speech and held
a challenge in their eyes.
Some looked afar, brows furrowed.
A woman sucked her lower lip,
blinking back her sorrow.
Whites talked above a whisper,
gave their Black brethren space.

Holding a mug of coffee, my taste ruined
by too many cigarettes, I stood
next door with neighbor Richard raking his 'fro.
He joined other Black men walking
toward Dixwell Avenue for an impromptu march
in protest to New Haven's Green. I followed
to lend witness to their grief.

Two hundred Black men lined two-abreast
outside the Monterey and trekked
the mile downtown. I kept pace,
in my place across the street, and saw
people step aside, raise a fist, bow a head.
The priest at St. Martin's held hand to heart.

Black leaders mounted a platform
at parade's end and spoke: "All whites
to the rear. Move back. It is time."
Moving back, I spotted a white acquaintance.

He nodded. I nodded. We walked back
together. We knew our place.

I heard the men on stage give voice
to anger, loss, to grief and pain.
Racist hate wrought a national disgrace
when Martin Luther King was slain.

Crushed

Arthur the Hat offered free booze
to all at New Haven's Park Plaza to hear
Bobby make his pitch in '68.
A free taste and a glimpse of the great
man compelled my presence. The packed
ballroom confirmed Art Barbieri's political genius
in matching martinis with the Kennedy charisma.

Bobby ran late. I clipped a drink
from a passing waiter's tray, chatted up Libbie,
the beautiful Black stewardess
in her TWA red shift minidress,
and her gal-pal, Barbie, with the blond mop top.
Libbie loved Bobby. Barbie had a crush.
I might get lucky. One might settle
for me after the Senator left.

Word spread the man had arrived.
We three made for the hallway
to catch a close view of the next president.
A few men and many ladies lined the crowded corridor.
A phalanx left the elevator and walked the gauntlet
to high-pitched screams of "Bobby!"

The cordon collapsed
when frantic women converged on Kennedy.
I found myself suspended and crushed
against the ballroom doorjamb by Bobby's back.
The grasp of security saved the senator.
He vanished, cocooned by their bulk.

I fell to the floor and gazed up at the women's faces.
Smiles turned to scowls. Hopes crushed,
realizing their prey had fled,
the women left the hallway.

Flat on my back, with no broken bones,
I rose and stumbled into the boisterous ballroom
to find my female friends had lost me in the crowd.
Abandoned, I searched for a waiter with a tray of drinks.

A Truncated Trip

MacTriff's featured jazz at night.
The day gang preferred rock.
If the bartender lagged in playing 'Trane,
the jukebox treated us to something by The Beatles.
The bartender's bum knee slowed him, so friendly fortune
let the sunshine in with a whole lotta love
for the grand rock tunes of '69.

Martha and Pam entered the bar on that Saturday
in mid-August. They would often come together.
Ever energetic Pam crooned that they
would drive their bangles and beads to Woodstock,
boyfriends at work be damned.
This event could not be missed.
Who would join them? Not I. Like the boyfriends,
I had a job. Lovely leggy Martha and Pam
in peasant blouses found four pilgrims
from our everyday people to join their journey.

Six sturdy souls loaded their van with eats and drink
and left New Haven near noon. We welcomed
the respite, dimmed the lights, sat in a silent way,
and mellowed with Myles. The van parked,
back on Chapel St. before dark.

Withered from wine, wasted from weed,
Martha and Pam entered the bar, none too nimble.
The van overheated in Derby before the flat in Danbury.
Not feelin' alright when they crossed the Taconic,
Pam yearned for the boyfriend's bell-bottoms.
The bartender mumbled something
about the creator has a master plan.

Winchester's

I make what kills our enemies in war.
A married man and father must provide.
The job lets me meet needs and share some fun
with kids and please the wife. I can't complain.

The pay does not alone comprise job's joys.
My pleasure in works' friends extends beyond
the gates of Winchester Repeating Arms.
At Christmas parties, card games at the club
on Henry Street, we take a break from when
we make what kills our enemies in war.

The certitude with which I've done my job
to help our boys bring evil to an end
is questioned now, in '69, by those
whose voices I respect. These last few years
have merged the voices of the anti-war
with those of civil rights. Since Nixon won,
but not Connecticut, Winchester's lost
its contract, as of January first,
to make what kills our enemies in war.

The thought of people I have helped destroy
makes losing work much easier to absorb.
In looking where to earn a good week's pay,
I'll want to work where I will have some say.

Minnesota Strip

I remember how I had awakened after midnight.
Stabbing chest pains seared each breath.
My lungs burned with the heat of fires, magnified by dread.
I hustled my worried not-yet-thirty ass
down to the New Yorker hotel's three-story lobby.
The concierge heard my problem. "French Hospital."
He pointed to the revolving door to 8th Ave.
and allowed, "a few blocks down and to the right."

Across 34th, the hot humid July '69 night turned meaner yet.
A blast like winter warmth shot from a subway vent.
Young women patrolled the Farley building.
Neither heat nor gloom of night stayed their appointed rounds.
Hot pants and leatherette micro-mini hovering
above calf-high spike-heeled boots, one woman lay
supine across a coral and white Edsel coupe's wide bonnet,
breathing in rhythmic regularity of deep sleep. A dark man,
in a black tee and khakis, offered, "My man, want a girl?"
"Not now, I need a hospital."
"Turn right at 30th. Can't miss it."

The sleep deprived doctor finds nothing
wrong in two hours of tests. He tells me to turn
off the window air. Relief, a six-foot wave,
sinks the disturbing suspicion of a heart attack.

I glide from the hospital up the avenue on a cloud of relief.
The sleeping beauty still adorns the hood of the decade-old car
across from the Garden. "My man,"
the cheerful greeting comes. "Want a girl, now?"
"No thanks, sleep will do." Still shaky from my scare,
I choose to forego the proffered favors of the flesh.
In the cavernous hotel lobby, the lone night clerk studies
sheets of paper and doesn't raise his eyes.

Take Five

A slender man,
slicked-back hair,
black case—violin, pool cue,
machine gun?
walks in near October '69 closing time.
The lone drinker downs his shot.
I wipe soiled shredded rag
over dregs of drinks from sinners
gone from MacTriff's to late night's
summons of excess.

Piano Mike nods to stranger's request.
Black case, once opened, yields tiny shiny sax.
The quivering reed on bandstand belies
a birdless night. Notes fly
straight to souls of bar keeper
and two couples still seated at tables.

Catchy chirpy repetition of "Take Five,"
Paul Desmond's iconic jazz tune,
causes waitress to stare and stand still
in wondrous stupor.
The barfly spins
his stool to see.
Bass and brush drums slide
toward stunned silence.
Mike lays an upbeat line of reverence.

The solo ceases and the man and horn leave
the astonished us too few for proper homage.
"Mike?" I ask.
He looks and shrugs,
"Desmond, passing through."

Panthers

Playing touch football on Carmel St.
with Norman and Warren, who knew
the law would tap my phone? Turns out,
Warren and Ericka, Norman's sister in law,
figured prominently in New Haven's Black
Panthers of the late sixties.

Maybe, they tapped the phone because Joan,
my next-door neighbor, left her law school
husband for a local Black Power activist.
Then again, eavesdropping on our racially mixed
marriage might have supplied kicks
sufficient to the law's cause.

Neighbors and I organized voter drives,
challenged the political status quo, tended
more toward MLK than Huey Newton.
We would stop our basketball game to watch
Floyd Little boom punts at Beaver Pond Park.
Lawful progress, not revolution, defined our aims.

Our home on Orchard St. sat a block
from Panther headquarters, where torture
transpired, and people planned murder.
The trial shocked and split our tight circle.
The end of this decade of sexual and social
awakening left us searching for solutions,
pondering which paths to pursue.
It promised turmoil untold.

About the Author

William X. Conlon studies creative writing in the MFA program at Southern Connecticut State University where he also earned his B.A. degree in liberal studies. He retired from the active work force after an eclectic entrepreneurial career. Bill lives with his wife, Debbi, and their tuxedo cat, Sylvester, near the beach in West Haven, Connecticut., where he ponders the wonders of life while watching the tides ebb and flow.

Order more copies of Speaking of the Sixties

Contact
William X. Conlon
wxconlon@gmail.com

$10 each book

$3.00 Shipping and Handling

Flying Horse Press
West Haven, CT

9 798718 385892